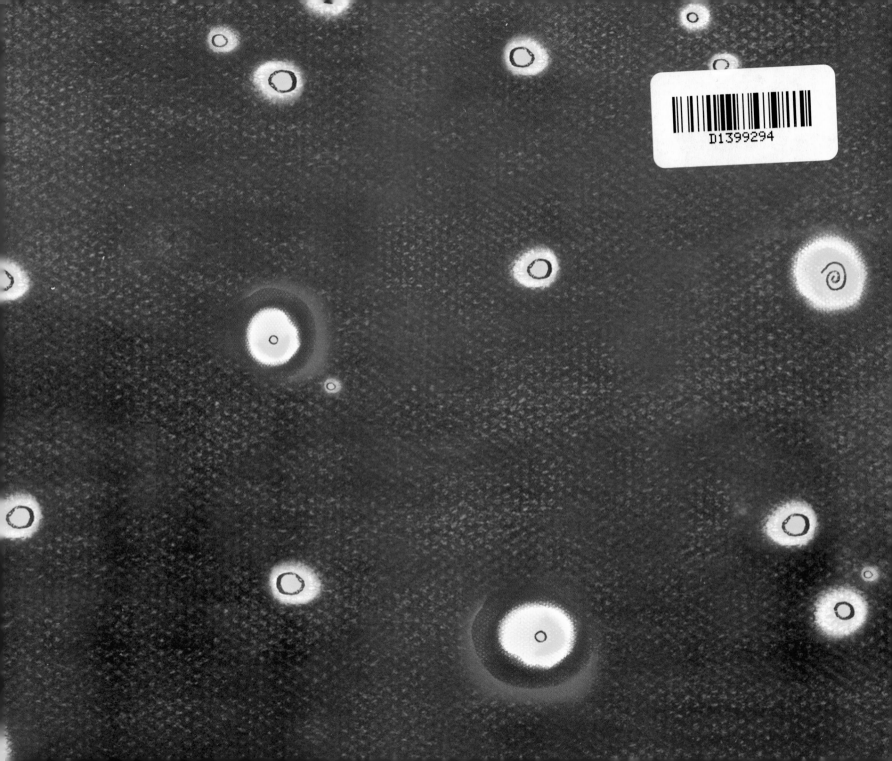

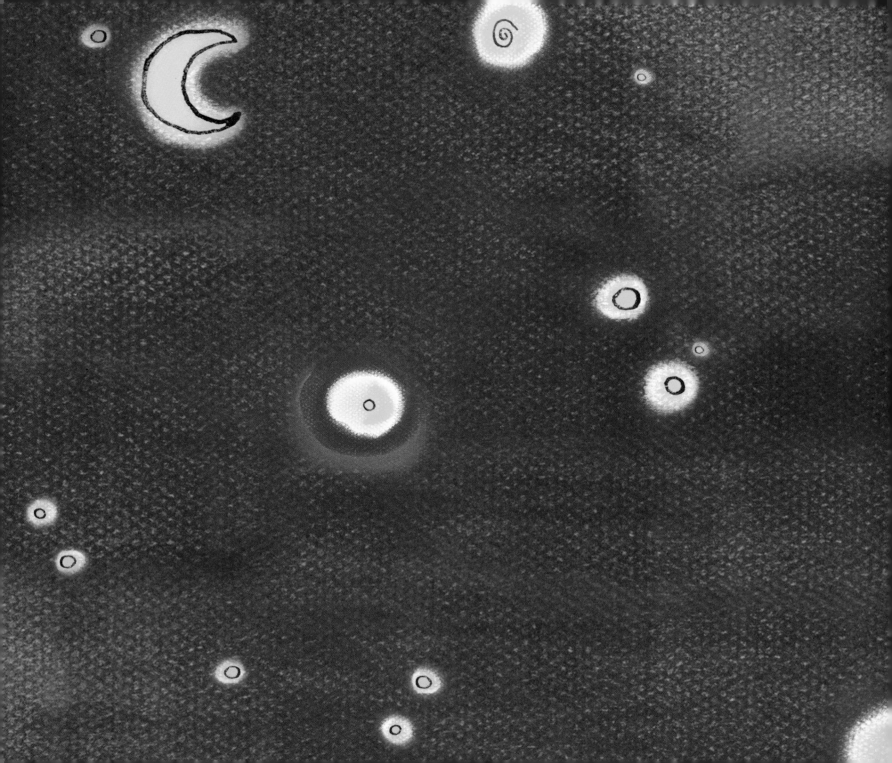

Nightlights

More Bedtime Hugs for Little Ones

by **Debby Boone** illustrated by **Gabriel Ferrer**

HARVEST HOUSE PUBLISHERS
EUGENE, OREGON 97402

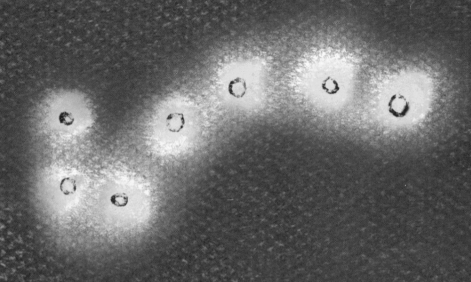

NIGHTLIGHTS

Copyright ©1997 by Resi, Inc.
Published by Harvest House Publishers
Eugene, Oregon 97402

Library of Congress Cataloging-in-Publication Data

Boone, Debby.
    Nightlights / Debby Boone and Gabriel Ferrer.
        p.   cm.
    Summary: A collection of short pieces about lights at night,
including "Candles," "Fireplaces," and "Stars."
    ISBN 1-56507-734-2
    1. Children's stories, American.   [1. Light—Fiction.   2. Night—
Fiction.   3. Short stories.]   I. Ferrer, Gabriel.   II. Title.
PZ7.B64593Ni   1997
[E]—dc21
                                                       97-12443
                                                          CIP
                                                           AC

Design by Koechel Peterson & Associates, Minneapolis, Minnesota

Printed in the United States of America.

97 98 99 00 01 02 03 04 05 06 / BG / 10 9 8 7 6 5 4 3 2 1

At the end of a busy day, when the dinner mess is finally cleaned up, the kids are bathed, toys are put away, and your energy has gone over into the negative, you still have ahead of you some of the most important time you will ever spend with your child—bedtime.

Some of my fondest memories come from the bedtime rituals I grew up with. The whole family kneeling by the side of a bed to say our prayers. Good night hugs and bedtime stories. And on occasion, convincing my mother or father to lay by my side for "just a few minutes…"

I now know firsthand from several years of bedtimes with my own four children both the fun and frustration, the joy and sacrifice that bedtime can bring. There have been nights when I didn't know if I had anything left to give, but my own childhood memories were all the motivation I needed. I want my children to have the same kind of memories and to grow up experiencing the kind of love I was so privileged to grow up with. My prayer is that when they are raising children of their own, they will want to pass on these same bedtime traditions.

It is my hope that *Nightlights* can contribute to the fun as you create some of your own family's bedtime memories.

Debby

nightlights

Some people don't like the night time
because it's dark and sometimes a little scary.

I do.
I really do.
You know why?
Nightlights.

I don't mean the little lights
you plug into the wall so your bedroom
doesn't turn pitch black
(but I really do like those...)

I mean all the nightlights...
stars twinkling
candles glowing
city lights
moonbeams

Don't you think they're beautiful?

Did you ever notice that you can't
really see any of those things
during the day
and if you can...
they're really not as pretty?

We don't really appreciate light in the daytime

but when it gets dark
we realize how much we need light
and how much we really love it.

I like night time.

city lights

One of my favorite things
in the whole world to do at night
is to drive up the hill by my house
and park
and look down
at all the city lights.

It's like lifting up the top
of an old dark chest
and discovering the most valuable treasure:
priceless jewels sparkling in all different colors
rare gold coins
precious pearls.

One night
I realized that all those lights
are part of people's lives.

Now I like to try and figure out
which light is the house where my friend lives
or which light is the store where I buy my favorite ice cream.

One of those lights hangs outside
the shop where that nice man fixed my bike.
I wonder which one is the pet store?
(I bet the mice in there are all awake and playing.)

Everything I will do tomorrow
and everyone I will see
is hidden in those city lights each night.

Just like hidden treasure.

dreams

What is the one thing you can only do
when you're sound asleep?

Yep, that's right.
Bingo!
Good answer!

DREAM

While your body's asleep
and getting all the rest it needs,

it's like a light goes on
inside your brain
and a dream version of you
is busy doing all kinds of different things.

Sometimes I wish you could choose your dreams
like you choose which book you're going to read.

Hey, I like surprises as much as the next guy,
but sometimes you have bad dreams
you'd just like to forget
and sometimes you can't remember
dreaming at all.

I like adventure dreams
where you are the hero and get to save the day
or dreams where you can fly.

I've had some pretty swell dreams
I wish I could dream over and over again.

Maybe if you think about it really hard
before you go to sleep
you will dream your favorite dream tonight.

stars

Why has everyone
who has ever lived
in all of history
in all of time
looked at the stars?

Why do we love stars?

Is it because they twinkle like diamonds?
(like the song says)

Is it because we can count on them to always be there?
(even when the clouds cover them)

Or is it because...

stars are what we wish upon

and they remind us
that there are as many possibilities
for tomorrow
as there are stars in the sky?

So make a wish

and close your eyes...

flashlights

I like to keep a flashlight near my bed
so that I always have light when I need it.

But from time to time a flashlight
can also be lots of fun.

If you take a flashlight
under the covers
and make a tent

you can pretend you are out in the wilderness camping.

This is especially fun to do with
a friend or a brother or sister.

And while you have someone
under there with you,
put the flashlight in
your mouth

close your lips around the top of it
and your cheeks will light up all red
like a scary monster.

You can push the light against the inside of your hand
and on the other side you can see all your bones and veins.

Or you can just lay there on your back
and make the light dance on the ceiling like Tinkerbell.

And when you're through,
turn off your flashlight
and put it somewhere close by.

And you'll sleep a little better
just knowing it's there.

glow in the dark fish

Deep deep down in the sea
way way down
(much deeper than you can hold your breath)
it gets darker and darker.

And if you could go down even further
you would see some strange things.

You would see some fish.

And because these fish live so far down
where there isn't any light at all
they carry their own lights with them.

I don't mean flashlights or lanterns...
I mean lights that are built right into
their bodies.

Some of them have lights above their eyes...
Others have lights all down their sides...
And some can just make themselves glow all over.

Imagine that!

I bet if we never stop looking for them
the world will never run out of surprises.

Like fish that glow in the dark.

lighthouses

Lighthouses have one purpose:
to shine their light.

Some really big ships
don't have much need for lighthouses.
They have special stuff
right inside their boats
to tell them where to go
and how to avoid danger.

But smaller boats
depend on lighthouses when it's dark
to keep them from harm
and to point them in the right direction.

I think moms and dads are like lighthouses
and children are like the small boats.

We can depend on moms and dads to take care of us

until we get big enough
to have the special stuff inside
that we need to take care of ourselves.

Maybe one day you'll be a lighthouse.

tooth fairies

Have you ever seen a tooth fairy?
I haven't.
But I have seen the money they leave.

You know, when you lose a tooth,
and you wrap it up in a handkerchief,
or put it in an envelope?
And the next morning...
wow!
money!

I think there are lots of tooth fairies,
because everyone I know
who has ever lost a tooth
tells a different story.

Some tooth fairies leave notes,
and some don't.

Some give five dollars for the first tooth,

Elliot

Cheapskate Wally

and fifty cents for all the rest,
some leave a dollar a tooth,
and some really cheap t.f.'s
just leave a quarter.

No kidding, I know someone
who got TWO HUNDRED DOLLARS
from a tooth fairy in North Carolina
for one tooth!

I'm not sure if there was something
really special about that tooth,
or if that tooth fairy was a little crazy.

But I think I'm going to make sure
my teeth stay nice and shiny...
and if I ever get to North Carolina
I hope I have a loose tooth.

candles

I love candles.

All kinds of candles.

tall graceful ones
tiny little ones
big fat ones
short candles in different colored glasses

Have you ever noticed
that even the simplest candle
is beautiful the moment you light it?

Candles are for special occasions.
like birthdays
holidays
parties

or maybe just because
someone special is coming to dinner

Sometimes just lighting a few candles
makes an ordinary night
a special occasion.

Candlelight has the nicest way
of making everything look beautiful—
a magical way of looking
for the good in a thing
and making it light up.

That's what love does.

Don't you love candles?

windows

Do you ever look into
the windows of other houses
as you're riding in a car at night?

Or do you live in an apartment building
where you can see the windows
of all the different apartments across the street?

I don't mean to spy on other people
(that wouldn't be right)
but just to look at the lights
to see a table or a bookshelf
and to wonder...

...wonder what those people had for dinner
...wonder what books they are reading
...wonder if they like the same kind of ice cream that you like.

Do any of my neighbors have a crazy dad
who sings songs and plays loudly on the piano
while his children laugh and dance all around?

Are any of my neighbors like me?
And how are they different?

I'll tell you a secret...

sometimes I ask myself these questions
when I look into other people's eyes.

I've heard it said
that the eyes are the windows of the soul.

I wonder.

fireplaces

Fire can be scary and dangerous...
it can do a lot of damage.

But when it's in a safe place
—like a fireplace—
it can be one of the
most wonderful
things that I can think of.

It keeps you warm and
cozy on a cold
winter's night.
It smells so good in
your house and
outside, too.

You could almost
    watch it forever...
as the flames dance in all
    different colors
and the wood crackles
    and pops as it burns.

It seems like whenever there
    is a fire in the fireplace,

that's where everyone in the
    house wants to be.

Faces glow around
    a fireplace—
and you can watch the
    flames dancing in
    people's eyes.

When fire is in a safe place
    like a fireplace
it has a way of making
    everyone feel
that they are also
    in a safe place...
like a home.

fireflies

In certain places
at certain times of year
and only for about an hour...
just as the sun has almost gone down

there is something very special in the air:

Fireflies.

I wish I lived where there are fireflies.

But I'll tell you one thing...
no one was ever more excited than I was
when I went to visit my grandparents
    in Tennessee
or my cousins in Virginia
during the summer.

I practically held my breath until it started to get dark
and with my nose squished against a window
I would look out over the lawn until...

flash.

flash.

flash.

And out the back door I would run
to jump and laugh
and dance the firefly dance.

I'm glad God made fireflies.

angels

I'm not exactly sure how it works with angels.

But I like to think about them...
especially at night.

What do they look like?
Are there different kinds?
Are there men and women angels
with great big wings?
(like some pictures and statues)

Or are they like those pudgy little babies
with little tiny wings?
(like you see on valentines)

Do angels show up sometimes looking like a normal person
to help us when we just can't seem to help ourselves?

Some people say they have seen angels.
I never have.
(and I don't really know anyone who has)

But you know what I think?
I think angels don't really want us to see much of them
because they don't like to draw attention to themselves.

I think they just like to remind us
that God cares about us
and is always ready to send a
little help our way.

Like on the wings of an angel.

inside light

Has something been bothering you today?

Did someone hurt your feelings?
Or maybe you said something
you shouldn't have said
or did something you shouldn't have done.

It's hard to go to sleep
when something is troubling you, isn't it?

Feelings can be hard to talk about sometimes.
But if you keep your feelings inside
it's like being alone in a dark closet.

If you can talk to someone
(especially someone who loves you)
it's like turning a light on
inside you
and you discover you are not so alone.

Someone once said,
"Two heads are better than one."

But two hearts
that share their deepest feelings...
now *that's* something very very special.

So, try it next time something
    is bothering you.
Turn on your inside light.

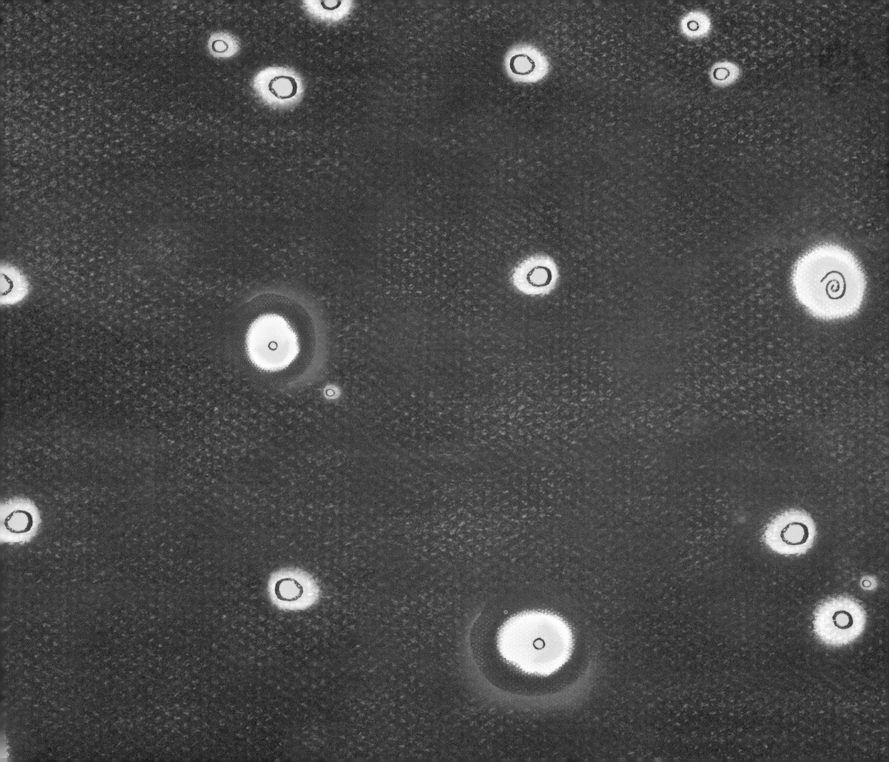

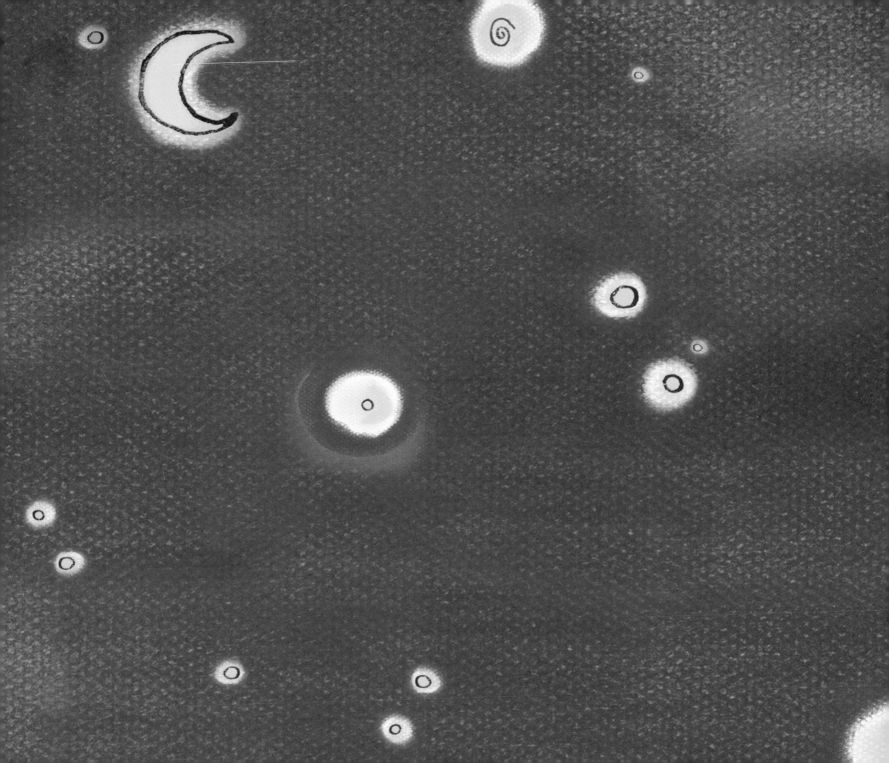